A Rookie reader

Quiet Wyatt

Written by Larry Dane Brimner
Illustrated by Rusty Fletcher

Children's Press
An Imprint of Scholastic Inc.
New York • Toronto • London • Auckland • Sydney
Mexico City • New Delhi • Hong Kong
Danbury, Connecticut

For Carson and Cassidy Brimner.
—L. D. B.

For my boys, Will and Sam, who are seldom quiet,
but are always the best part of my day.
—R. F.

Reading Consultant

Cecilia Minden-Cupp, PhD
Former Director of the Language and Literacy Program
Harvard Graduate School of Education
Cambridge, Massachusetts

Cover design: The Design Lab
Interior design: Herman Adler

Library of Congress Cataloging-in-Publication Data

Brimner, Larry Dane.
  Quiet Wyatt / by Larry Dane Brimner; illustrated by Rusty Fletcher;
reading consultant, Cecilia Minden-Cupp.
      p. cm. — (A rookie reader—opposites)
  ISBN-13: 978-0-531-17543-9 (lib. bdg.)   978-0-531-17777-8 (pbk.)
  ISBN-10: 0-531-17543-X (lib. bdg.)   0-531-17777-7 (pbk.)
  1. English language—Synonyms and antonyms—Juvenile literature.
I. Fletcher, Rusty. II. Title. III. Series.
  PE1591.B74 2007
  428.1—dc22   2006027034

SCHOLASTIC, CHILDREN'S PRESS, A ROOKIE READER, and associated logos are
trademarks and/or registered trademarks of Scholastic Inc.
1 2 3 4 5 6 7 8 9 10 R 17 16 15 14 13 12 11 10 09 08

In a loud, loud town
is a loud, loud street.

On this loud, loud street
there is a loud, loud school.

And in this loud, loud school stands quiet, quiet Wyatt.

Why is Wyatt so, so quiet?
Can he roar like a lion?

He can roar like a lion.
But today he's quiet like a mouse.

Can he howl under the moon?

He can howl under the moon.
But today he's as silent as the stars.

Can he rumble like thunder?

He can rumble like thunder.
But today he sounds as soft as
one tiny raindrop.

Listen to Wyatt roar like a lion!

Hear him howl under the moon.

Cover your ears when he rumbles like thunder!

But not today.

Usually there's no one
louder than Wyatt.

But sometimes it's
good to be quiet!

Word List (58 words)

(Words in **bold** are used as opposites.)

a	him	no	**soft**	thund
and	**howl**	not	sometimes	tiny
as	in	on	sounds	to
be	is	one	stands	tod
but	it's	**quiet**	stars	tow
can	like	raindrop	street	und
cover	lion	**roar**	than	usuc
ears	listen	rumble	the	whe
good	**loud**	rumbles	there	wh
he	louder	school	there's	Wyc
hear	moon	**silent**	this	you
he's	mouse	so		

About the Author

Quiet Larry Dane Brimner is the author of many titles in the Rookie R series, among them *Here Comes Trouble*, *Raindrops*, and *Cats!* He also the author of *The Littlest Wolf* and *Subways: The Story of Tunnel Tubes, and Tracks.*

About the Illustrator

Rusty Fletcher works from his home studio in the historic village of Granville, Ohio. Rusty feels lucky to be able to do what he really love create artwork for children's books. He has two boys of his own, Will Sam, who are sometimes quiet and sometimes very, VERY loud.